Copyright © Roland Cam

Copyright © Chris Lambert

The right to be identified as author has been asserted by the authors in accordance with the Copyright, Designs and Patents Act 1988.

All rights reserved. No part of this publication may be reproduced, stored in a retrieval system, or transmitted in any form or by means, electronic, mechanical, photocopying, recording, or otherwise, without the prior permission of the author.

A CIP catalogue record for this title is available from the British Library.

All characters in this publication are not fictitious, any resemblance to any real persons, living or dead, is as presented by the recorded memoires of Mykola [Michael] Spiwak - deceased.

ISBN –

Hell Hides in Many Hollows

The Co-Authors

Roland Cam

Roland Cam is a 'pen name' as this author prefers and values a measure of privacy and anonymity. Roland has seen active service as a member of the Armed Forces before becoming a peripatetic teacher

Roland has a B.Sc [Hons], and two post graduate degrees and includes a Psychology degree, and teaching qualifications for teaching in Adult, Higher, Secondary and Primary Education.

The author has written and is currently editing three books – The Cult of the Dead, Sorceress of All Rome, and The Pact of the Troika. He is also a Freeman of the City of Chester, and was listed in International Who's Who for work with Adult Learners in 2002.

Chris Lambert

Chris is a successful businessman and a much valued, popular and respected member of the business community in Leeds, and elsewhere.

Mykola [Michael] Spiwak was Chris's Grandad, and it was Chris who first recorded the recollections and memoires of Mykola Spiwak, between 1997 – 2022.

Chris is also a highly qualified and extremely skilled artist and tattoo artist. His 'A' List requires no further elaboration.

Both authors are agreed this true story is one of historic, sociial and personal interest, and also relevance in a world where the Ukraine is still struggling for the right to live and govern autonomously. The lessons learned from previous conflicts should not be overlooked and forgotten – especially for future generations who may know nothing at all of the true horrors of war for civilians as well as for its protagonists.

Forward
Chris Lambert

I promised my Grandfather I would publish his memoires one day. It was a promise I always intended to keep, and not just because he was my Grandad and I had always been very fond of him.

As a grown man, I felt enormous anger at the story he'd unfolded before me. It's almost incomprehensible that such a level of suffering could be inflicted on so many people by a small number of empowered individuals.

The anger never left me. I feel it still.

It's as if we never learn.

I believe there is a point where all educated people must recognize our elective silence is an indifference that makes us all complicit. There is a point at which we must ask, how can this still be happening?

I have real concerns that the lessons we ought to be learning from the true experiences of people like my Grandad are not, even now, widely known. Nor can they be considered sufficiently - given the level of devastation wars continue to inflict on so many people, around the globe.

With the recent events in the Ukraine and the very real threat of all of us being drawn into a war with Russia, it seems an appropriate time to finally be publishing my Grandad's story.

It may be that in some circumstances a handful of wars really cannot be avoided. But History suggests - time and time over - most can be.

My hope is that we will recognize more fully the level of suffering wars so often inflict on the innocent. May we finally begin to address the systemic inadequacies that allow a few individuals to impose these horrors on so many.

We have but one life. It's beyond precious.

We need to be ever vigilant, with our eyes wide open to the tools of propaganda, deception, false narrative and nationalism and ever more mindful of the unseen costs of war, as well as the ghastly horrors it delivers on the front line. I believe these are the important thoughts my Grandad wanted to share.

When we lose sight of our compassion for other people, we throw away our humanity and much of the value it holds.

I want to thank Roland Cam for the way he has represented my Grandad's best intentions for us all. Together, we share in the deep hope that others may read my Grandad's story, and take something of value from it.

My sincere thanks also to those people who have helped with proof-reading and commenting on this work.

We both felt it was a story that really should be told, at a time when many of should be grateful that the Ukraine may be the obstacle to yet another invasion into Europe.

Contents

Chapter 1	Just the Beginning	8
Chapter 2	Betwixt the Hollows and the Promises	15
Chapter 3	Two Wrongs Don't make a Right	28
Chapter 4	From Pillar to Post	32
Chapter 5	What Next?	38
Chapter 6	Weaving Our Way – Through Bradford	46
Chapter 7	The Golden Years	51
Chapter 8	Michael Spiwak's Message to Us All	63
Chapter 9	Thumbnail Photographic Library	65

Chapter 1

Just the Beginning

He was laid out in bed because he was dead. In the Ukraine it was traditional.
Through the open doorway, my grandmother seemed entirely calm as she washed him down.
I suppose when life is mostly severe it becomes just another cruel challenge to be faced and overcome.
She covered him with sheets, and the visitors calling in, were many.
My grandad's brother and my uncle carried him out in the coffin, before leading the two horses and the cart down to the wooden church, which was catholic, rather than orthodox. Not that it mattered. Most of Demnia turned out to pay their respects.
At the time the village boasted about a hundred houses and my uncle, who was a joiner, had built much of the church himself. It's still there.
I watched them lower the coffin into the ground. The driven rain helped to hide my tears as the cold reality of it all bit a little deeper. My memories of happy times with my grandad went back to when I was about four years old. He always had time for me, as I did, for him.
My father took over as the head of the family. The handweaved garments he made with flax held great value locally, and he'd sit up on many nights making clothes. Some paid him in Polish zloty. Others worked off their debt by working on our family farm. It was the only way to get clothes if you were poor - and most were.

I'm old now. It's strange how some memories remain so vivid, while others are forgotten or sketchy. I'm the only one left, so far as I know. Of all the boys I grew up with, I mean. Some of them were shot by Russians, others by Germans, and old age claimed the few that were left.

The 'school' was based in a rented house in the village, and one large room became the only classroom. There were never enough children of age to fill all the places. I first went there, when I was aged just four. My brother was two years my senior and he looked after me.

It was winter when they first opened our village school. Often, we were snowed in, and it was always very cold. Sometimes my uncle carried me there, to see me safely through the snowdrifts.

The sole teacher was a Polish man, and he was as fierce as he was harsh. It seems that in 'good education' there is little that cannot be embedded a little more firmly with a few cane strokes across the knuckles or buttocks – most frequently, with no articulation of prior learning required.

School was every day for four hours in the morning.

My afternoon duties were to graze the two cows in our fields.

Farming; Location and year unknown.

From 1917, the Communist Party had gradually increased their hold in Ukraine. Demnia is fairly central within Ukrainian land mass. At first the communists controlled mostly the eastern side, while parts of the west were divided between Poland, Romania and the former Czechoslovakia.

When the Germans invaded Poland in September of 1939, the communists responded by occupying the rest of Ukraine more thoroughly - right up to the border with Poland. I would have been about 12 years old, so I was probably born in 1927. *

Communist pledges to improve the standard of living in Ukraine were but empty words, and most natives resented their intrusion. The soldiers that came to our village were arrogant and often boasted about how great and wealthy Russia was. In reality, they had nothing, but their self-deception was strong.

They came to 'keep watch,' There was soon talk of local people who spoke out or who broke the 'new rules' being sent to Siberia to work in the salt mines.

On the day they came to confiscate our cows 'for the good of the party,' my mother was fearless. 'How will I feed my children?' She demanded, and I saw the Russian woman waiver under her distressed protests. I thought they might arrest her, but the KGB woman eventually relented and took the soldiers away with her. Perhaps it was all just too much trouble?

I was always curious about that. Why did they always believe that the way to create something better involved making the poorest poorer? There was rarely consideration for the impact taking the animals away would have on the farms they looted from.

In Ukraine you lived on what you could harvest from the land and the animals. If the crop failed you went without, and few could afford to replace livestock, when they were taken.

[* Marie Spiwak has indicated that Michael more usually gave his date of birth as 18th February, 1926 in later years. It was not unusual, in Ukraine, for people not to be sure - in the years leading up to the war].

They must have known, by then, it wouldn't be long before the Nazi's from Germany replaced them as the occupying power in the Ukraine. Perhaps they thought my mother's fearless resistance was best left for the advancing Nazi's to contend with?

As far back as the 15th and 16th Centuries, Ukraine was occupied – then by Poland. In 1772, the Austrians annexed a part of the Ukraine but mostly it was under Polish control.

The Polish people took the houses and the jobs. The native Ukrainians were seen as lesser people, left to survive on what they could grow and provide for themselves.

Later, Poland struck an agreement with France to help the Poles take back full control. In return the French received supplies of Ukrainian oil and gas.

It seemed Ukrainians were always kept poor despite the huge wealth embedded in their Ukrainian soil.

My dad always spoke with great pride about his time in the Austrian Army. He had been sent to wage war against Russia and when a shell landed, nearby, he was wounded and buried in soil. The Russian Revolution had begun around this time, and he was captured and put into a Russian POW camp in Moscow.

Somehow, he managed to escape and he walked all the way back to his home in the Ukraine. [615 miles].

After only two weeks he was drafted into the Ukrainian Army, and was again taken captive, this time by the Polish Army, who kept him as a prisoner in a cellar.

It was shortly after he was released and returned home that he met my mother. Together they raised a family of four boys and a girl.

Chapter 2

Betwixt the Lies and Hollow Promises

It was the summer of 1941 when the Germans came. The initial fighting with the Russians took place elsewhere. Hitler attacked Russia and demanded they withdraw from Ukraine. The Russians gave way and moved back into Eastern Ukraine, taking their tanks and troops with them.

Before the Germans did arrive, local people whispered 'The Germans are coming,' and we became suddenly fearful about what the future might yet hold.

The mountains and the forests around the village became a training ground for the Ukrainian Resistance Movement, who were preparing to confront both Russians and Germans.

I saw a man walking past the farm late one night. He was dressed in a dark suit. 'Where are you going?' I asked.

'To see my girlfriend on the other side of the village. One day, you will have a girlfriend on the other side of the village, too.'

I knew I was too young to join, and I knew he was lying. It was the worst kept secret in the village.

Everyone knew they were meeting in the forests around the village.

They were simply villagers who felt they had to resist and did eventually progress to killing Germans, destroying train lines and stealing weapons and munitions.

The German response was to round up people in the villages they suspected of being involved and shoot them on the spot.

The village school had closed in the winter when the war started. There was nobody to pay the teacher's wages, and he fled back to Poland. That was before I saw the German tanks and trucks passing on the main road.

The Poles, we knew, had their own resistance movement but they wouldn't link up with the Ukrainian one, and at one point they regarded each other as enemies.

That year, when the Germans came, there was very little food in the shops. The river had burst its banks and floodwaters destroyed most of the crops.

We had some cabbages, carrots and potatoes – but not much else.

It was very likely that people were going to starve that year.

There were seven people in our household, including my parents. We knew the food we had wouldn't be enough.

On my 17th birthday, my father suggested that we should go to Lviv, where the Germans had promised there was plenty of paid work we could do. We agreed that he and I could go and earn to send money back to the family to see them through the shortages.

My little sister, Maria, was just eighteen months old when we left.

Lviv was fifty kilometers away and we left on 17th February, travelling on foot.

On the first night we stayed with relatives in a village on the other side of the river, and walked all of the second day to try to get to Lviv.

We were very tired and stopped at a house to ask for directions and food. The villager could only offer us some warm water to drink. She told us the nearest train station was just two kilometers further.

During the war you didn't need train tickets, but you had to get a permit to travel.

We waited at the station all night. We had no food left. The chicken we had prepared was not enough for the whole journey.

The Gestapo office at the station opened at 9am. My father spoke some German as he had been in the Austrian Army for a time. The Gestapo said I was too young to be employed in Lviv, but they let me travel as I was with my father. They wrote the passes.

The train arrived at 10 am and an hour later we found ourselves at a Sleeping Camp.

There were no beds and no tables. Just a very dirty floor to sleep on, in a wooden barrack building. The toilet was just a deep hole in the ground. If you'd have fallen in, you'd have drowned.

We were given half a loaf of bread to last the week, and there was only tap water to drink.

My father was sure he knew the barracks from his time in the army.

It was three weeks before our names were called out to join the train for the next leg of our journey.

There was no food or water for this part of the five-day journey.

The train crossed the Polish border before heading up to Austria through Czechoslovakia, stopping often because the German troop convoys had priority where rail met with road.

Mostly, we sat in silence, wrestling with our own thoughts and hunger. I seriously thought I might die of hunger before we reached our final destination.

Eventually, we stopped at a Prisoner-of-War camp. It was huge. We saw Polish, British and American troops held there, through the wire that segregated us from them.

The first queue was to storehouses where we had to tie our clothes into a small folded bundle. We wrote our names and addresses on a piece of paper and trapped it under the string.

The second line took us to cleansing chambers where we were gassed to kill off any bugs we might be carrying.

The next line took us to shower, and then we queued naked, to be examined by four separate doctors. They shaved my head, and we filled out papers and they recorded my details.

After about half an hour, we were told to go back and find our clothes.

I had a suit, and a shirt, but no socks. My shoes were home-made by me. I also had some leather uppers from an older pair, into which my uncle, who was a joiner, hammered wooden pegs to attach them to the wooden soles and hold them together. These were now my winter shoes.

In Ukraine, there had been no shops where you could buy metal nails.

The line for food on our side was enormous, too. We queued with our plates held out eagerly, watched over by a German sentry with an Alsatian that growled continuously, and wanted to bite everyone.

When food came, finally, it was one scoop of Macaroni.

The next morning, we boarded another train. The journey was a mountainous one that took us on to an Austrian town, where our overnight accommodation was to be inside an enormous and empty civic building.

There were no beds, but at least we had warmth for the bitterly-cold night. There was also a hot cup of tea but no food.

It was an early start the next day, and the train took us to Regensberg. Again, there was no food. Not even a hot drink.

That evening, we slept in an empty house in a village – this time in a wooden bed, before completing the shorter journey on to Munich, the next day. In all, it had taken the larger part of four weeks.

We lined up in a large empty building, while owners of factories and farms inspected us. A farmer looked my father up and down. 'You'll be good to work on a farm for a lady I know,' he announced. My father replied in some German, and that seemed to seal the deal. Her husband and sons were away fighting, leaving her with the farm to manage on her own, he told my father.

The same farmer then asked for me by name. He said that I would be good 'forced labour' for his own farm which was quite near to where my father would be set to work. It was to be my job to help graze his own cows.

We looked around at the hundreds lined up. We were the only two chosen at that session - and so it was that my father and me ended up working apart, but on farms quite close by.

On the farm I attended, there were already three Polish workers and another, from France. There was also a young Polish girl who helped me tend to the cattle. It was left to the other workers to show me around the farm, and to introduce me to the cattle and to the two bulls I'd be watching over, as well.

In the morning, there was a slice of bread each, and a coffee substitute, made with Barley, to drink. My duties were feeding the animals and mucking out, along with any other 'occasional jobs' the farmer found to be done.

On the second day, the shared task was 'muck spreading,' aided by three carts with two horses for each. The day was a seamless cycle of filling the carts up, spreading the load across the fields, and then re-filling the wagons. We worked until nightfall.

Lunch was another slice of bread with a small amount of butter on it.

It wasn't too long before I heard that my father had been moved. The lady's husband and three sons were all killed, in close proximity. He was sent first to a factory in Munich where his task was to spray paint tractors. But he was moved again, shortly afterwards. This time, they sent him on to the Hungarian border to help dig trenches, but the expected Russians, never arrived.

After two years, and now aged 18, I was moved on too. They said I was now too old to be tending to the cattle. I was now on a farm in the next village, where the farmer had absolute confidence that the Germans would win the war. He was very unpleasant to work for, and very ignorant.

I was joined by two Polish workers, and a French prisoner of war, also sent to work there.

The senior farmer was fiercely proud of the family members who were in the high command of the Nazi Party. He was also convinced that I was only aged about fifteen years, and not eighteen. He made it very clear he did not much like me because I looked 'too young.'

Fortunately, the farmer carried injuries from the First World War, and he used two sticks to help him walk. So, there were days when he wasn't around – or so I thought.

On the first occasion the older farmer wasn't there, his son barked orders at me and shouted in language I didn't follow. He was a large man, and he punched me in the face when I answered back in my own language.

I saw stars and nearly fell over.

'Speak only in German when you are here,' he ordered.

He shouted at us a lot, and I learned quickly not to answer back.

He was just as nasty as his father.

Farming. Location and year unknown.

Despite these early setbacks, I stayed at the farm until the war ended, by which time I was the lead worker, working with horses and ploughing the fields.

Shortly before the war ended, in 1944, one of the Polish workers was loaned to a nearby factory in Munich. It was not unusual for farm workers to fill temporary vacancies in this way.

While working at the factory, the Polish worker stole a watch, and the police were informed. Worse still, the police found the watch in his wardrobe after he returned to the farm.

He ran away after they found the watch - knowing he'd be arrested. For several days, he hid inside the hay stacks on a nearby farm, stealing food there, to survive.

He was found eventually, and they took him to court, where he was sentenced to be hung. They also sent him to jail to await execution, but it was a cold day in February, 1945, before they got around to the hanging.

On that day, the Gestapo came for us too. They thought we should watch him hang – as we'd worked with him – and as a caution to all of us. There were five Gestapo, and two men from a local Concentration Camp who acted as executioners in return for extra food. I don't know what nationality they were, but you could see they were better fed from their ruddy complexions. We were all sallow and pale from being undernourished.

Now, at the woodland space they took us to, there was confusion as to why we did not all have 'Pear' patches on our chests. They thought we were all Polish workers, and all Poles carried this mark on their chests.

They began to beat us, but I was able to hide between two larger men. There must have been about a hundred workers taken there to witness the execution.

I escaped the beatings.

I didn't want them to discover I was Ukrainian, or they'd have sent me to join the Ukrainian Army and to fight on the side of Germany. If the Russians had caught me in Ukrainian uniform they would have shot me. Neither did I want to die fighting for the Germans, whom I really didn't like at all.

The two 'executioners' hammered extra pieces of wood onto a tree to secure the rope, while the Nazi's pushed us all into position to watch. The prisoner stood precariously, legs shaking, on a chair – with the noose already around his neck.

The Gestapo head reminded us all why this was happening.

'Anyone who steals will be hung,' he warned us. 'And now you will pay attention to see fully what this means.'

[The irony of their own involvement and purpose in the war must have momentarily eluded them! Or is occupying other countries somehow not stealing?].

They nodded to the two POW's who kicked the chair away. The prisoner clutched desperately at the rope tightened about his neck, kicking, dancing and convulsing on the end of the rope for a full two minutes. His tongue came out of his mouth almost down to his knees.

'This is what will happen if you steal,' they announced.

The dead man stopped struggling. It was grotesque.

When we got back to the farm, the farmer's daughter asked 'Well? Did you enjoy it?'

'No!' I told her fiercely.

She changed her tune and her manner. 'They shouldn't have hung him! Then, he shouldn't have stolen either.'

They wouldn't allow the convicted man's burial in the local cemetery, alongside 'decent' Germans. They left the body in a ditch beside the cemetery wall – as a reminder.

From that day, every time I closed my eyes to sleep, I saw images of the man being hung – legs kicking, with his enormous, strained tongue and bulging eyes. It looked like his head was going to burst! It took a long, long time for the images to stop – at least three months. Even now, my wife tells me I have nightmares, and she believes I am still re-living the war in my head. I think my brain shuts the memories out from the moment my eyes open.

Chapter 3

Two Wrongs Don't Make a Right

A Russian family were sent to work on the farm at the beginning of 1944. They disliked the German farm owners almost as much as the farm owners disliked them.

When the end of the war looked to be in sight, the elder farmer asked me to take the Russian family away to one of the empty camps, about two hours away, by car. They were as glad to be leaving as he was to see them go. The farmer was so pleased, he paid me 15 marks to take them, and also gave me some Hospital Stamps.

The farmer told me his son – the one who had hit me – had been compelled to serve in the German Army for the last few months of the war. He had avoided earlier service because the daughter had married the most senior Gestapo officer in Munich. There were none more senior, in fact.

Two weeks later the son turned up back at the farm.

He told me he was a 'changed man' and he felt sorry for us, and began to treat me well whenever I saw him. He told me 'Hitler was a liar' and the Germans were not winning the war.'

'Do you think they can win?' He asked me one day.

'I don't know.' I told him, as speaking against the German forces carried a death sentence.

'It's okay.' He assured me. 'You can say. I won't tell anyone.'

I said nothing. I still had no trust for him.

The next thing I overheard was he had completed his 'leave' but deserted from the German Army. We guessed he was hiding on his girlfriend's farm in the next village. He knew then that the American tanks were not far away.

I now practically ran the entire farm.

I worked with the horses, day and night – often working a twelve-hour day in the Winter months. In Summer, it was regularly a sixteen-hour day.

The Americans came and some stayed at the farm, briefly. It was only after they had gone that the son reappeared.

When the Americans first arrived at the farm, they came at night. They asked who we were. The American officer in charge was of Polish descent and could speak the language. I told him that the owners were 'bad' people and how they'd made us sleep in the stables with animals, only once cleaning our sheets. He told us we had been held illegally. He ordered the owners to be shut in a pen with the chickens and handed me a pistol.

'In twenty-four hours from now, they will be meeting to sign a treaty ending the war. You can take your revenge- if you wish, but if you do kill them and it is discovered, you will risk jail after the treaty is signed,' he said, leaving it to me to decide the fate of the family.

I looked at the German owners. They huddled together, in the corner, crying. They were sure I would kill them.

I was eighteen or nineteen years old at this time. I felt great anger at them but I was not a killer. I handed him the pistol back and told him so.

The Americans told us to pack and to head straight to a refugee camp that was being set up. Some of the workers didn't want to leave, fearing they would be sent back to the Ukraine which was still occupied by the Russians. Perhaps they thought they would be punished as collaborators. Most were delighted to be free.

I danced and sang all night, singing in my Ukrainian mother-tongue. I was so glad to be leaving the slavery of the farm. When I had gathered my few belongings, I just left. I didn't say goodbye to anyone.

Chapter 4

From Pillar to Post

It only took five minutes to walk to the farm where my father was, but much longer to resolve our choices. My father wanted to return to the Ukraine. '

'No way,' I said. I didn't want to become a communist, a Russian soldier, or to work in a dirty factory.

A reminder of his time in a Russian Prisoner of War camp during the First World War made him reconsider. It was possible that the Russians still had a record of his name, and good treatment suddenly seemed unlikely.

We left together. There was little for us to carry. We headed for the Displaced Person's (DP) Camp I'd dropped the Russian family at.

We called at a warehouse on the way. We'd heard you could get repaired German soldier's boots. Most had holes in the soles that had been plugged with wood, but we searched hard and found some good ones.

The DP camp was full of people from many different parts of the world. Most had very little in the way of belongings, except for the Russians.

The Dutch were the first to be repatriated. They were quickly replaced by more people from the Ukraine and Poland, but we managed to take over the Dutch barrack room.

We'd been there for two nights when the Russians began shooting at each other. The arguments were mostly about girlfriends. One night I heard bullets whistling through the corridors. It seemed that one Russian had killed another about a mile away, near to a river. Only he'd come back to tell the girlfriend what he'd done, and then he fled.

Other Russians found the body and buried it in the middle of the camp.

Eventually, someone told the Americans, and a Lieutenant arrived with soldiers. He called them 'Barbarians.'

'Haven't you seen enough killing?' He asked, angrily. 'Now you are killing each other!'

The Americans left and went in search of the murderer.

Food parcels came from Britain and America, each week. There was a small loaf of bread, and if you were lucky there was tinned food. Very occasionally we might even get some butter, but we ate less often in the DP camp than when we worked as forced labourers. On the farm we'd eaten a small amount three times a day. Here, there was never enough food to go around.

It was around this time that I noticed I was losing my sight in one eye. There was no medical help available in the camp, so I caught a train and went into Munich.

A doctor inspected my eye and could see nothing wrong with it. The equipment was too old to show anything of value.

'I'll have to take your eye out,' he told me.

I went back the next day, and he 'popped' my eye out using a metal spoon. It seems extreme now and it hurt a little, but I wanted the problem sorted out. It's what had to be done.

I could see my eye hanging there through my good eye. That was a little disconcerting.

They examined my eye for a good five minutes, before putting it back in, but could find nothing wrong.

'Come back tomorrow,' they told me. 'There will be an American doctor in charge and he's very experienced with eye injuries.'

I did as they asked.

'You've burst a blood vessel at the back of your left eye,' he confirmed. 'I cannot treat it fully, but I can give you something to help.'

He arranged for me to visit his own surgery at the American barracks in Munich, where he had more advanced equipment.

He gave me an injection in the back of my eye. It was very difficult to treat, and he wrote me a letter so I would be able to pass on the right details if I moved away from the area. It didn't seem to help very much and I went blind in one eye.

Back at the DP camp, the Americans did what they could to repatriate people, but it was a slow process. The Russians left next, followed by the Polish people there. Most Ukrainians didn't want to go back to a Russian occupied Ukraine.

There was now more room in the camp, and although a large number of Polish people arrived, we were able to organise the camp in a better way.

We allocated rooms and organised a proper kitchen. The food management was improved and we now had cleaning rotas. We even had a camp committee to represent the Ukrainian and Polish groups.

It was a further year and a half before we were moved. This time, we were sent to a camp in Hindenburg in Augsburg. It was a Ukrainian only camp with about ten thousand occupants.

I was invited to become a policeman to the camp by the Americans. They sent me to Regensberg for two weeks, where I was trained in Judo, general police duties, and how to make an arrest. There was no pay for doing this work, but occasionally I'd be given a couple of packs of American cigarettes.

Michael took an unpaid job as a
police officer to the camp

The night shifts were a struggle. I found it hard to stay awake. As well as general police work, I was expected to guard the hospital door, and also an illegal Vodka factory maintained by the camp owners. As a reward for guarding the large vat of vodka, I was allowed to dip a big ladle and drink as much as I could in one go. I couldn't take any away with me as there were no containers to carry it in, and taking alcohol into the camp area wasn't allowed. The ladle full was large enough to ensure I got drunk, even so.

We were transferred again, this time to the 'Old Town' in the Schongauer region. The camp was much smaller here with only about fifteen to sixteen hundred occupants, and we remained there for about a year and a half before being moved to Mitten Wald, in the Alpine peaks of Bavaria.

Mitten Wald was a lovely town and we stayed there until February in 1948.

Chapter 5

What Next?

Britain opened its doors offering paid work and housing just as Belgium closed theirs. The USA was also an option but it seemed too far away, and about eighty of us were like-minded. Britain it was - on the train, of course.

On the station platform, I met a Belgian girl I had seen at the dance the night before we left. I'd been struck by her beauty at the time, but there were so many drawn around her I hadn't asked for a dance. She was travelling with her mother back to Belgium, and she confided that she found me very attractive and tried to persuade me to go to Belgium with her where we could marry.

When I turned down the idea of going to Belgium, she told her mother to continue without her as she wanted to travel to Britain with me, so we could marry there. I didn't oblige.

There was also a man I knew from my village in Ukraine. He told me my oldest brother, George, had been drafted into the Russian Army. (They shot you if you didn't agree to be enlisted). He also told me George had been wounded in one foot, and they'd sent him home.

It was now 1948. I didn't know I'd never see George again. He'd taken a job on the railway but died from throat cancer before I had a chance to see him.

My father moaned a lot. He wanted to see my mother and his family. I reminded him that as soon as we reached the border at Ukraine, the Russians would split us up. Reluctantly, he agreed that Britain was the better choice – for now.

There was the problem still of somehow altering his age on his papers. He was now aged 59 years old but we needed him to be 50 so we would both be young enough to join the workforce and be allowed to emigrate to Britain, together.

I found a Ukrainian woman who said she could alter the papers, but it would cost 1,000 German Marks [About £91 in old Sterling].

There was no work near to the station so I set about 'fiddling.' When I say 'fiddling' I mean the well-known three cup game, where a ball is hidden beneath one cup, and then the cups are mixed quickly so the gambler loses track of which one it is hidden under.

The Archway beneath the station was the perfect spot. We stayed there, too. German prostitutes sold themselves cheaply under its apex for a slice of bread, and so there was rarely a shortage of young men there.

I made a point of only taking a profit from Germans. My fast hands deceived them every time.

One day, I sold a jar of Nescafe coffee to one German – except we'd added brick dust to make up for the coffee missing from the jar. I couldn't believe it when he came back the next day asking for another jar 'only without the brick dust.' He must have realised what we'd done.

Sometimes, we'd take a train into Munich to see a show.

It took about a year and a half to get enough money together to alter the papers.

We were all set to leave when we discovered we had to wait for another fortnight before we could be taken to Munich on an American truck.

In Munich, we had a narrow bed in another camp, and were seen by an American doctor. I was completely blind in one eye by now, but the doctor passed us both as fit for work. We waited for a train to take us to Hanover in the British zone. In the end, we stayed for another fortnight and then we were put on a train to Holland. Finally, we were put onto a ferry bound for Dover.

At Dover, our papers and bags were checked and I was given one pound in Sterling. A load of bread was just 4d – four old pennies, but the money would have to last me a very long time. From there, a train took us into London where we were put into a functional hotel, but at least it was clean.

Breakfast was a delight with a slice of bread and a rasher of bacon. It didn't fill you very much, but we were glad of it.

The next day began with the same breakfast but we were quickly herded onto buses bound for Cambridge and an empty POW camp. From Cambridge we were able to get a bus up to York and yet another POW camp.

I was given another pound note but our wait lasted for another four weeks before we could move on with our intended journey.

There was another medical at the holding camp in Cambridge. My damaged eye meant I couldn't be sent to work in a mine. Instead, it would be farmwork. I was given a choice between Scotland, or further South. I chose the latter and was sent to a farm in the Midlands, between Banbury and Northampton.

There were about thirty of us, and we travelled by train to a POW camp in the area. From there daily trucks took us out to our respective farms, and brought us back at night.

The camp had been cleaned up by the Army, and we began to settle and organise our life there.

On the farms, most of the work we did was about putting irrigation in place for crop plantations, so we dug a lot of ditches. The frequency of work was very irregular. Sometimes we were needed just for a day, and at other times it could be a full week.

This was the pattern for three years, and we were contracted to the government. The pay seemed okay at first, at £5 a week – but by the time you'd paid the utility bills and food bill, we'd be lucky to save £1 a week.

We also had to provide our own shoes and suits.

We were told that we could buy clothing quite cheaply at the Market Place in Northampton, but when we got there, we discovered you had to have coupons to buy anything. We only had our savings in cash.

A Jewish stall holder helped us out by selling us coupons and then accepting them back in exchange for clothes. Strictly speaking, it wasn't legal, but at least we could get what we needed.

Our camp was in a rural area and so buses were very infrequent.

Having shoes and suits transformed our lives. We bought sports pedal bikes at £16 each, and once booted and suited, we were allowed to go into local dances at Woodford, and elsewhere. My bicycle was great. I loved my new freedom. Imagine our disappointment to discover most of the local girls didn't trust 'foreigners' at all.

A £16.00 bicycle was 'life-changing.'

I remember a time when I was so drunk I couldn't ride my bike, and my friends had to carry me home. Another time, I'd taken a bus to Northampton and met a beautiful Irish girl who was very keen to go the pictures with me. Sadly, I felt Northampton was too far to travel to all of the time. I could see no future in the relationship, but on that occasion, I managed to miss my last bus. The taxi fare home was very expensive.

Author's Note; *The sums of money mentioned seem to imply that it was possible to save more than just £1 Sterling. But an old pound was worth 240d, or old pennies, and many items including beer were still priced in old pennies. A pack of ten cigarettes was 6d, and a pint of beer was 1 shilling and 2d - or fourteen old pennies. There were twenty Shillings to a £1 and a Shilling was worth 12 old pennies.*

When our three-year contract was completed, we were at liberty to work wherever we could find work. My dad had been employed in collecting up land mines along the east coast.

I received word my dad had suffered a nervous breakdown. He needed help quite urgently but I didn't have the money to get to him. The police had found him, travelling aimlessly around by train. He spoke hardly any English but they found his papers and traced him to me through the UK Ukrainian Committee. They'd put him in jail for the night, not knowing what else they could do with him.

The Army put him back to work picking up mines. He had another breakdown, and they took him to hospital.

I was told it was very likely he'd be sent back to Germany as he hadn't completed his three-year contract.

At the hospital I asked him why he'd been riding around on the trains.

'I was looking for you,' he said.

I stayed at the hospital overnight, and we left for Bradford the very next morning – together.

Chapter 6

Weaving Our Way Through Bradford

In the 1950's and 1960's, Bradford was a boom town. It already boasted the largest Asian population anywhere in the UK, having recruited workers to fill the jobs in the wool mills. At the time, the Ukrainian community was about five hundred strong.

Many of the workers from Northampton travelled with us in search of work. We settled in Manningham, where five of us rented and shared a single bedroom, with just two beds.

We found work in a wool mill at Baildon, but they didn't want to give my aging father a job at all. They agreed to take him on if I'd work there too. They re-set a loom to run more slowly for him, as his mental health was no better. I worked extra hard to make sure we were valued. Alas, the work lasted only for a year, as there was a wool shortage, and we were both made redundant.

Still! It was good while it lasted.

There were then four dance halls in Bradford, and I used to visit them all, and have a few drinks in the evenings.

I had a tailored 'Teddy suit' and the Cameo Dance Hall became my favourite.

Our suits were always blue, grey or black, with a long jacket and drain pipe trousers. I used to buy a new tie every couple of months. Yellow, green and blue were my preferred colours. The Crepe-souled shoes were a key feature of our 'uniform.' Unfortunately, my hair was beginning to fall out at this point, so
I'd cut it short and try to hide the gaps by brushing it forward. The many years of poor diet had to show up somehow, I reasoned.

This was where I met my future wife, Marie. She'd bop away in a corner with no shoes on, and her three friends did the same. They'd just left school.

Michael & Marie Spiwak   Marie Spiwak [1955]

17th September, 1955

I'd sometimes walk her home, as our streets were fairly close to each other. She was already dating a Ukrainian when first we met, but he emigrated to the USA to fulfil his ambition of joining the US Army. So, it was a good year and a half before we began to date properly.

Marie travelled to Germany to see her boyfriend and tell him they were finished. He promised to marry her, but he'd already confided in me that the Army was 'his life.' She didn't trust his promises either.

I married Marie when she was 21 on 17th September, 1955 in the Registry Office at Manningham. Our reception took place at Buzby's Restaurant. It cost us £36 to feed 40 guests and £9 for the Wedding License.

We paid for the reception as her mum found she was unable to keep her pledge to cover the cost.

We managed to get a mortgage on a property in Manningham, and Linda, our first child was born in 1956, followed in 1958, by our son, Stephen.

I'd taken a job at Laing's Builders, creating new blocks of flats.

A regular part of my job was lifting heavy concrete loads using an electric pully system. One day the brake failed. It turned out that someone had dropped a huge concrete chunk onto the brake motor unit, and not told anyone. The metal cable holding about one ton of concrete snapped and the lashing cable whipped past my head, missing me by about an inch. I was lucky to be alive.

Incidents like this tend naturally to promote a measure of reflection, and I concluded that the pay level really didn't justify the risk. So, I left, just as soon as the new building was completed.

In 1963, I did die. Briefly, anyway!

I'd collapsed on my way home from work and was coughing up blood. The hospital at Middleton tried to work out what was causing the bleeding.

Apparently, I just stopped breathing and they couldn't revive me.

When I came to, I was on a cold, metal table with a sheet over my head and body. I had no idea how long I'd been there.

'Help,' I shouted.

A nurse came in from a neighbouring room. 'I'm so glad you're alive,' she told me. 'We've just finished writing out your Death Certificate.'

A porter took me back to a proper bed. His name was Cheshire. I didn't know then he'd turn out to be my daughter's future father-in-law.

They say 'You only live twice.' My daughter nicknamed me '007.'

Michael Spiwak – probably in Bradford post 1955

Chapter 7

The Golden Years

I took work with Nelson's, the builder's, repairing factory and church roofs. It was a good job for two and a half years. Then, one day in Wetherby, where we were repairing an old cottage, we all went for a lunch time drink at the pub next door, and played Dominoes. But the boss passed by and saw us all sat outside the pub. Drinking was strictly forbidden, and we all got sacked 'on the spot.'

Michael [Mykola] took a building job

The 'Golden Years' came early in my work, at least. I found my way into other work at Sandoz on Canal Road at their chemical plant. To begin with my job was to propel the 'bogie' [a hand propelled rail truck, as seen on old Western movies, sometimes] around the factory dropping off chemicals where they were needed.

They moved me onto a night shift making chemicals for the textile industry, and I got to be really good at it. When the new factory was built at Horsforth, I moved with them, as by now I was able to mix any of the chemicals needed. I liked the new factory for its cleanliness and for how 'modern' it looked.

When a supervisor quit, the management team invited me to take the job. I didn't want the responsibility but they urged me to take on the new role managing thirty-three workers in one half of the factory, and things went well for the thirty-three and a half years I worked there, until my retirement.

In my last five years there, I was moved over to managing the tankers – cleaning, filling and preparing them for deliveries. I had a team of twelve, and we worked shifts between us. It was around this time that the Textile Industry was sent spiraling into decline and all operations moved to Japan.

I retired in 1991, aged 65 years, and have suffered a number of illnesses including four heart attacks. I'm grateful to the NHS for my many years, having outlived all my brothers, and reached the age of ninety-three.

My father had died in 1973 having never qualified to draw a pension. The lie about his age cost him dearly, as you needed about forty years of full-time work to qualify for one. He died without ever having returned to the Ukraine – although he did send some parcels to my brothers there.

I'm not sure my brothers ever received the packages he sent. The KGB there were corrupt and charged people in Ukraine, to deliver them.

I recall he sent fabric from Bradford so my brothers could make a suit. It never reached them. They couldn't afford the delivery charge and the KGB confiscated the tailor's sewing machine, anyway. The KGB confiscated anything of value.

In his later years, my father's mental health continued to decline. He'd visit neighbouring Ukrainian families and frequently complained I was not 'a good son to him.' I tried my best to keep him out of a nursing home but eventually we had to find him a place in one, and it seemed better than a mental health institution. He became a 'difficult man' in his declining years, although never a danger to anyone else.

The Community Centre was very much a part of who we were.

When he died, I saw that he received a traditional Ukrainian burial, and I think people concluded I wasn't such a terrible son after all.

My own health improved when I was given tablets and Radium treatment for my damaged vision. I produced the letter written by the American doctor all those years earlier. The treatment was very quick, and although I suffered from painful headaches for a time, my vision cleared and the problem never returned. I was very grateful for it.

Marie and I still went dancing together, in our retirement, then in 1992, we managed to have a five-week holiday in Canada. We also took my Grandchildren away to Disney World.

On another occasion, we took a fortnight long cruise to Greece, Israel and Egypt and visited Christian holy sites in Israel before touring the tomb of Tutankhamun, and others in Egypt.

I enjoyed our visit to Jordan, and the Holy Land, immensely. We also went to the Catholic church in Bethlehem where Jesus was christened. There was a silver star represented on the floor and pilgrims and priests from the world over came there to kiss it. offering pilgrimage prayers.

As a part of the same tour, we were taken to visit a Jewish Gold factory where they also cut diamonds. It was full of shops selling jewelry.

That night when we got back to our ship, I wore a white tuxedo, and Marie and me danced all night to a live band. They're great memories that comfort me still.

Officially, Ukraine gained its independence from Russia in the Gorbachev reform years on 24 August, 1991, but it wasn't long before Boris Yeltsin was claiming it as a legitimate part of Russia again. I don't think the Russian's will ever let go of the Ukraine or the Crimea. And now we see history being repeated all over again under Putin.

The Black Sea belongs to Ukraine, not Russia.

I recall the Ukrainian Rebellion in Kiev when I'd watched it on tv. How they'd shot a hundred people who voiced peaceful opposition to those who wanted to rejoin Russia, and how the 'puppet president' fled to refuge in Russia, shortly after. His personal mansion was shown, showing the corruption of it all.

You'd think after four hundred years of Russian oppression there'd be more objection, and, as recent events have shown, actually there is.

I watched an account of a mother begging her son not to join the Ukrainians fighting off the Russian supporters - but he was determined to free his land. He was back within a week, wounded, and deeply changed. As he lay dying while his mother served his last breakfast.

She wept and cried out in her own hurt and anger at the stupidity of Ukrainian killing Ukraine, only too aware of how powerless poverty left all Ukrainians. Losing her son to such a tragic cause was too much to bear.

I had begun to write to my brothers in Ukraine but I always feared for them under Communist rule. They could be sent to jail, shot, or sent to Siberia, and so I was always wary about what I wrote.

As you might expect, I have no liking for Communists or Nazi's. They're both extreme – and that's where the problems begin for so many people.

The last time I had seen my own family was in 1942. Finally, three years after the Berlin Wall came down, I was able to return. It was 1993. I felt great anticipation for the journey, but it was not without some very significant disappointments, too.

The attitude of the security guards at Ukraine seemed 'almost Russian.' They tried to intimidate travelers into paying them cash to let their bags pass unsearched. I told one of the officers I had no money in my case and he simply passed it through.

I did give some money to one of the customs officers - as he was the only one who made no effort to coerce any from me. When he declined to accept, I thrust it into his hand.

It was an attitude that came as a great disappointment - although there was no denying their obvious poverty, either.

I remember the feelings of sadness I felt.

It was all complimented by the attitude of the customs officers at Poland, later, who seemed quite determined that all 'Ukrainians were thieves, smuggling out the treasures from their native country.'

It's what happens whenever extremism gains a foothold. Why was I surprised?

I'd hoped somehow things might be very different to my faded memories, but the poverty persisted. The airport had no lights on, and we crossed the tarmac with sludge and running water beneath our feet.

We were met at the airport by one of my brothers and his three sons. I couldn't remember what he'd looked like and had no recognition of any of them. I had been seventeen years old when I last saw him.

We travelled back to the old family house in a rented Lada. The car was very old too. It bounced and shuddered at every pothole we encountered. The roads were in a terrible state.

At our family home, Marie asked to use the toilet, and my brother took her to a point in the garden where a plank was suspended above a hole in the ground. They had no need for toilet paper. A pig was always nearby to lick you clean.

Water came from a well but it was contaminated. Cleaning the well was too difficult, and the water source in use was a piece of pipe at the top of a hill where the water fell fresh and clean. Thankfully, it was very clean.

Ukrainians still ate what they could grow. There wasn't enough to sell. Colorado Beetle in the Potato crop had seen to that.

The shops were mostly empty, save for the old pop bottles occupying the top shelf with the sediment still at the top. I wondered if they were the same ones, after all these years?

Anyway, you needed coupons to buy anything, and they were controlled and administered by the local Russian or Ukrainian Mafia group, and could only be purchased with hard currency from a man who sat behind the blackened windows of his car.

The Russians had stripped everything. There was no education and no machinery.

Ukrainians queued up for a loaf of bread, but if the delivery didn't come, you went without.

The only contribution the Russians offered was to teach you how to become a KGB spy.

Everywhere we went was muddy. There was hardly any tarmac.

At the river, a wire was suspended so that you could pull yourself across in a small boat, and then continue your journey to our neighbouring village. Mostly people bathed in this river, using home-made soap created with meat fat. (I remembered how I used to swim here as a boy, and on one of my visits I braved the waters once more. It was wonderful).

The nearest proper shower was 20 miles away in Stryj.

In our own village, the orchards were contaminated by fallout from Chernobyl, and so the fruit was just left to rot.

We went to my mother's grave, in a hillside cemetery. She'd died in the war from illness. I was reminded that my sister had no understanding of death. Even now she was asking 'when my mother would be waking up?'

My sister had a vague recollection of my father leaving, but never understood why he'd left.

When my mother died from illness a few years later, she ran to the cemetery every day to cry at her grave. She was effectively left on her own, but went to school and spent a lot of time sleeping over at friend's houses.

Basil, one of my brothers, was employed guarding a Ukrainian Ammunition Store and he'd take food and visit her every other month – when he could, but eventually, the food and clothes he sent stopped coming.

When my sister was sixteen, she got work in Stryj – a nearby town. There she met her future husband and they had a boy together.

Sadly, her boy had a birth disorder and when he grew up he developed a drink addiction. He was often beaten up for 'womanizing' and unacceptable behaviours.

When her husband and son both died, she became deeply unhappy before finding refuge in the Christian faith. She finally found a place and acceptance in the Baptist Christian Church.

The shock of the level of poverty endured made a deep impression. We determined to continue our visits in the years ahead. As a result, we watched the changes unfold gradually.

On our second visit, there was more produce in the shops, but very few clothes. By the third visit, there were imported clothes from the West, and food could generally be purchased everywhere. But the Mafia exercised even greater control.

When three girls in our family group got married, people 'clubbed' together to lay on receptions in local amenities, like the school, and there was a traditional Ukrainian band, and people brought presents. Most recently, people now use hotels or restaurants, for these events. So, changes have been noticeable.

The Mafia presence has made the Ukraine a 'natural bedfellow' for the Russians. After all, corruption is rife.

It was on my third visit I met my youngest brother, Stefan. He looked very much like me, save that he had no teeth. He'd been sent to work in the Russian coal mines. Sadly, he died within three months of our first meeting.

When we returned to England, we found a Diamond Wedding Card from HM Queen Elizabeth waiting for us. It delighted us.

Nowadays, I take twenty-six tablets a day, and I rattle when I walk.

Chapter 8

Michael Spiwak's Message to Us All

My dream and my dearest wish is to see war eradicated. When will its madness stop? Politicians seem to thrive on it. All too often it's a pedestal to promote their own ambitions, or the ambitions of the wealthy, while the poorer classes pay with their lives.

The planet has enough available for us all to unite to live well.

Whether we believe in God in any formal way, or not, we must all see the value of supporting the morals that deliver a better life for everyone?

Much of the world is better educated, and yet we still engage in wars about petty religious differences, or wars driven entirely by the greed of a minority, in one way or another.

Even religion has become a pathway to riches just for the few.

Perhaps, if we shared a common language, we might reach a shared understanding so much sooner?

The greatest threat to us all, and to peace, comes from inequality.

I don't believe we can ever all hope to have exactly the same. There will always be some inequality. But there must surely be a 'better balance' between those who have so much, and the many, many more who have virtually nothing.

The poor in the world pay so much, while the wealthiest enjoy entirely better lives.

At the very least, addressing the inequalities should include greater parity in education, opportunity and standards of living.

There should also be a level of poverty that is rejected as unacceptable by everyone.

Perhaps when we finally make that our first priority, we can begin to create a better world for everyone – and not just talk about it.

Take the 'Party' out of Politics. Groups always tend to extremes. Work together. Unite against poverty.

This is my dearest wish for you all.

Michael [Mykola] Spiwak

18th February, 1926 – 13th February, 2019

Chapter 9

Thumbnail Photographic Library

The following photo 'thumbnails' are reproduced here for historical and social purposes, and also as a part of the record of Mykola's time with us, and before us.

THE TOWER
Blackpool

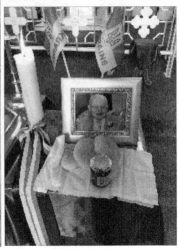

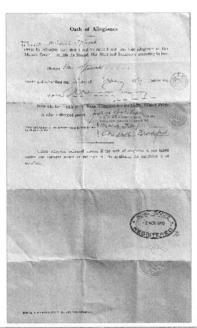

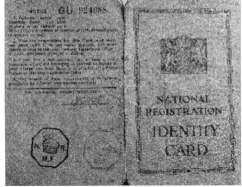

If you feel able to add to our knowledge about the photographs – especially who, where and when information, please contact Chris Lambert himself.

I hope you have enjoyed reading these memoires and looking through the photographs.

If you would like to produce something similar to this publication for a family member, relative, or friend, and you like this book, please contact Roland Cam at rolandcamwriter@gmail.com.

Personal Notebook

Printed in Great Britain
by Amazon

46755256R10046